THE WEAPONS ENCYCLOPÆDIA
TANK AIRCRAFT AFV SHIP ARTILLERY VEHICLES SECRET WEAPON

TWE-030 ENG

M4 SHERMAN USA TANK

THE WEAPONS ENCYCLOPAEDIA

EDITORIAL STAFF
Luca Cristini, Paolo Crippa.

ACADEMIC STAFF
Enrico Acerbi, Massimiliano Afiero, Aldo Antonicelli, Ruggero Calò, Luigi Carretta, Flavio Chistè, Anna Cristini, Carlo Cucut, Salvo Fagone, Enrico Finazzer, Arturo Giusti, Björn Huber, Andrea Lombardi, Aymeric Lopez, Marco Lucchetti, Gabriele Malavoglia, Luigi Manes, Giovanni Maressi, Francesco Mattesini, Daniele Notaro, Péter Mujzer, Federico Peirani, Alberto Peruffo, Maurizio Raggi, Andrea Alberto Tallillo, Antonio Tallillo, Roberto Vela, Massimo Zorza.

PUBLISHED BY
Luca Cristini Editore (Soldiershop), via Orio, 35/4 - 24050 Zanica (BG) ITALY.

DISTRIBUTION BY
Soldiershop - www.soldiershop.com, Amazon, Ingram Spark, Berliner Zinnfigurem (D), LaFeltrinelli, Mondadori, Libera Editorial (Spain), Google book (eBook), Kobo, (eBoook), Apple Book (eBook).

PUBLISHING'S NOTES
None of unpublished images or text of our book may be reproduced in any format without the expressed written permission of Luca Cristini Editore (already Soldiershop.com) when not indicate as marked with license creative commons 3.0 or 4.0. Luca Cristini Editore has made every reasonable effort to locate, contact and acknowledge rights holders and to correctly apply terms and conditions to Content. Every effort has been made to trace the copyright of all the photographs. If there are unintentional omissions, please contact the publisher in writing at: info@soldiershop.com, who will correct all subsequent editions.

LICENSES COMMONS
This book may utilize part of material marked with license creative commons 3.0 or 4.0 (CC BY 4.0), (CC BY-ND 4.0), (CC BY-SA 4.0) or (CC0 1.0). We give appropriate attribution credit and indicate if change were made in the acknowledgments field. Our WTW books series utilize only fonts licensed under the SIL Open Font License or other free use license.

CONTRIBUTORS OF THIS VOLUME & ACKNOWLEDGEMENTS
Ringraziamo i principali collaboratori di questo numero: I profili dei carri sono tutti dell'autore. Le colorazioni delle foto sono di Anna Cristini. Ringraziamenti particolari a istituzioni nazionali e/o private quali: Stato Maggiore dell'esercito, Archivio di Stato, Bundesarchiv, Nara, Library of Congress, Wikipedia, USAF, Signal magazine, Cronache di guerra, Fronte di guerra, IWM, Australian War Museum, ecc. A P.Crippa, A.Lopez, Péter Mujzer, L.Manes, C.Cucut, archivi Tallillo. Model Victoria (www.modelvictoria.it) ecc. per avere messo a disposizione immagini o altro dei loro archivi.

For a complete list of Soldiershop titles, or for every information please contact us on our website: www.soldiershop.com or www.cristinieditore.com. E-mail: info@soldiershop.com. Keep up to date on Facebook https://www.facebook.com/soldiershop.publishing

Title: **US M4 SHERMAN MEDIUM TANK - USA VOL. I** Code.: **TWE-030 EN**
Series by Luca Stefano Cristini
ISBN code: 9791255891666 first edition November 2024
THE WEAPONS ENCYCLOPAEDIA (SOLDIERSHOP) is a trademark of Luca Cristini Editore

THE WEAPONS ENCYCLOPÆDIA
TANK AIRCRAFT AFV SHIP ARTILLERY VEHICLES SECRET WEAPON

M4 SHERMAN USA MEDIUM TANK
USA VOL. I

LUCA STEFANO CRISTINI

BOOK SERIES FOR MODELERS & COLLECTORS

CONTENTS

Introduction 5
  - Foreword 5
  - Project 6
  - Technical specifications 16

Operational use 23
  - North African front 23
  - The war in Europe, Italy, France and Germany 25
  - The Normandy landings and the campaign in France 30
  - War in the Pacific 32
  - Korean War 37

Camouflage and distinctive marks 41
  - Last period 42

Versions of the vehicle 47

Conclusions 52

Data sheet 52

Bibliography 58

▼ The characteristic silhouette of the Sherman M4 on display here at the Novegro exhibition park (Italy).

INTRODUCTION

The M4 Sherman was the US Army's flagship tank, introduced in February 1942 as a response to the innovations in armoured warfare carried out in Europe by the Wehrmacht. The vehicle was designed to meet the urgent need to create large mobile armoured formations, and was equipped with a 75 mm cannon (later steadily improved over time) and two machine guns. It played a substantial role during World War II and later in the Korean War. Although the early versions suffered from a certain vulnerability, such as the ease of catching fire, the Sherman could boast one of the highest survival rates of the war among tanks.

The M4 Sherman soon became one of the most built tanks of the Second World War, with almost 50,000 units produced in 19 variants, sharing this record with the famous Soviet T-34. Thanks to its mechanical reliability and the versatility of its hull, the Sherman was also the basis for numerous other armoured vehicles, including tank destroyers and self-propelled vehicles, thousands of which were distributed (the latter will be part of a special volume on the Sherman). Almost all of the US allies made extensive use of them.

■ FOREWORD

At the start of the Second World War, official US Army doctrine maintained that tanks were to be used primarily in support of offensive operations conducted by the infantry. Instead, the destruction of enemy armoured vehicles was the primary objective of the so-called Tank Destroyer Battalions, equipped with anti-tank guns and self-propelled tank destroyers.

The American Sherman, capable of travelling long distances without serious damage, was a medium tank perfectly suited to performing manoeuvres aimed at penetrating deep into enemy lines. The US armoured units that landed in Normandy were mostly equipped with M4 and M4A1 Shermans, fitted with petrol-powered radial engines and 75 mm calibre guns.

In 1944, the M3 cannon mounted on the Sherman allowed the Allied crews to face the Panzerkampfwagen IV on equal terms, but the appearance of heavier German tanks, such as the Tiger and Panther, changed the situation drastically. It should be emphasised that during the conflict, armoured vehicle

▲ M3 tank assembly chain at the Detroit Tank Arsenal, Warren, Michigan (1942).

engagements were not the most common form of combat; in fact, tanks were more frequently involved in actions against 'soft' targets such as infantry, artillery or other unprotected vehicles. However, when the Allies began to encounter the Panther more frequently in Normandy, it became clear that the 75 mm Sherman piece was inadequate in the face of such adversaries.

The Panther could easily defeat the Sherman by hitting it from 1,000m. In contrast, the Allied tank's main armament could not pierce the Panther's thick and heavily sloped front armour, even at the shortest distances.

In order to remedy this problem, the British were the first to decide to increase the firepower of their tanks. The A30 Challenger, based on the Cromwell tank, was equipped with the powerful 17-pound (76.2 mm) cannon that boasted excellent anti-tank performance.

Nevertheless, the conviction emerged that the Sherman would be better suited to the fearsome weapon. The result of the conversion, carried out on the M4 and M4A4 variants, was the Firefly, which as of D-Day can be considered the most effective of the Shermans.

The Firefly's gun used three types of ammunition: armour piercing (Armour Piercing Capped), ballistic cap piercing (Armour Piercing Capped Balistic Capped) and high explosive (High Explosive). The Armour Piercing Capped Ballistic Capped projectile could penetrate a 13 cm thick armour plating inclined at 30°.

In August 1944, the new shell-piercing munition was available, which although it did not excel in terms of accuracy, was still potentially able to penetrate the frontal armour of the German Tiger II heavy tank at a range of about 1,500 m. The Americans rejected the British proposal to equip their tanks with the formidable 17-pounder as they were working on two new armaments, a 76 mm cannon and an excellent 90 mm piece.

▲ Several sandbags were placed on the front hull of this M4 (75) of the 3rd Armoured Division in order to provide additional protection against the German anti-tank portable weapons, the fearsome panzerfaust. Additional armour plating on the hull sides was added both during production and during the reconditioning of old Shermans. Stolberg (Germany), 3 November 1944. US NARA.

T6 medium tank, the Sherman prototype, USA 1941.

▲ Vintage World War II advertising image by artist GM Fisher in 1943 for Tank Art Dean Cornwell Military Decor, a well-known World War II magazine.

The M1A1 76mm cannon, installed on the new Sherman M4A1 (76)w and M4A3 (76)w, could at least theoretically knock out the Panther by hitting it head-on at a distance of less than 500m, provided the T4 high-velocity armour-piercing projectile with a tungsten carbide core was used. A small batch of M4A1 (76)w was initially distributed to the US 2nd and 3rd Armoured Divisions in late July 1944. Many American crew commanders, however, were reluctant to abandon their old Shermans because the high-explosive shell fired from the 76 mm cannon contained a far lower charge than the counterpart ammunition intended for the 75 mm piece. This would in any case change from January 1945 onwards. In order to increase the high-explosive firepower of the armoured units, the Americans developed two assault guns, the M4 (105) and M4A3 (105), and equipped the Sherman tank with a howitzer. Each US tank battalion in Europe would have been equipped, at least on paper, with six such armoured vehicles.

The British Army leadership, however, did not consider the use of Shermans configured in this way indispensable. Official US documents report that the British obtained 593 M4s (105) but it appears that none were actually used by them on the battlefields of north-western Europe.

The Three Rivers Regiment, operating as part of the 1st Canadian Armoured Brigade, was one of the rare Commonwealth units that had a limited number of these assault tanks in its charge, as evidenced by some photographs taken in the immediate aftermath of the conflict. The final version of the M4A3 (powered by a Ford engine), which was to equip the US Army for many years, received practically all of the main armament types envisaged for the Sherman (75 mm M3 guns, 76 mm M1A1 guns and 105 mm M4 howitzers) and also formed the basis for the M4A3E2, an assault tank whose turret boasted a 15.24 cm thick armour. Protection was further increased by welding additional armour plates to the upper hull, both front and side, and by the adoption of a massive new differential cover. Produced in 254 examples, the M4A3E2 was armed with the 75mm piece, which was more suitable for infantry support. Later, on around 100 of these tanks the original armament was replaced with a 76 mm gun.

M4A3E2s were deployed on the European front by the Americans as early as the autumn of 1944, and there is evidence that at least one of them was delivered to the 2e Régiment de Chasseurs d'Afrique, a formation belonging to the French 1st Armoured Division. In the United States, the debate centred on the role of tanks raged on until events on the battlefield made it unequivocally clear that the success of a fight depended to a large extent on the ability to employ an appropriate combination of infantry and armoured vehicles in the course of operations.

In 1942, the US armoured division was a unit generally intended to consolidate the success achieved by the infantry. According to the then-current US Army Organisation and Equipment Tables, it comprised two armoured regiments, both with three tank battalions, and a single mechanised infantry regiment mounted on half-tracks. This was a formation whose structure was strongly hinged on the armoured component, equipped as it was with no less than 232 medium tanks and 158 light tanks.

▲ A rare picture of the prototype of the first Sherman, at the time called Project T6. See plate on page 7.

Medium tank M4A1 'Major Jim' 2nd Battalion, 13th Armored Regiment, 1st Armored Division. Kasserine Pass, Tunisia, February 1943.

In September 1943, a new, more streamlined configuration was introduced, based on three tank battalions and as many mechanised infantry battalions. Each tank battalion consisted of three companies of Sherman medium tanks and a single company of Stuart light tanks. The division organised in this way thus showed a greater weight of infantry than in the previous period. In total, the 1943 model division had only 186 Shermans and 77 Stuarts.

Of the 15 American armoured divisions deployed on the European front, as many as 13 were of the 'light' type. Only the 2nd and 3rd Armoured Divisions retained the original, 'heavier' structure. Moreover, almost all of the independent tank battalions that participated in the European campaign were organised on the basis of the newer scheme.

Due to the limited war value of the Stuarts, battalions equipped exclusively with light tanks were essentially re-equipped with Sherman medium tanks.

The Army of Free France introduced three armoured divisions, the order of which was modelled on the corresponding US units. Each of the French divisions initially obtained 165 Shermans, mainly M4A2 (75) and M4A4 (75), versions that the Americans routinely allocated to other Allied forces engaged in Europe.

The French 2nd Armoured Division, part of the American 3rd Army, took land in Normandy only two months after D-Day. Although fully equipped with M4A2 tanks, it was also able to field some M4s (105). After suffering several losses in the summer of 1944, the division received, among others, Sherman tank models usually reserved for US units: M4 (75) and M4A1 (75) (primarily assigned to scout and self-propelled artillery units), as well as M4A1 (75) and M4A3, armed with 75 and 76 mm cannons or the 105 mm howitzer.

The French 1st and 5th Armoured Divisions originally had both M4A2s and M4A4s. In the course of the

▲ Interior view of the discreetly comfortable cockpit of the Sherman.

Medium tank M4(75mm), Company F, 2nd Battalion, 1st Armored Regiment. Tunisia, March 1943.

▲▼ Different types of engines used on American and British Shermans. From top left: GM 6046 diesel engine from General Motors. Right: a Ford petrol engine called GAA V8, superior in all respects to the Continental R975. Bottom left: the aforementioned Continental R-975 engine, an engine that underwent constant improvements to increase reliability and durability. Right: a Chrysler-multibanch M4 A4 engine.

Medium tank M4A1, Company G, 3rd Battalion, 13th Reg. 1st Armoured Division War Daddy in Tunisia, 1943.

European campaign, tank losses were replenished mainly with more M4A4s but also with a few M4A1s (76). Some Shermans equipped with 105 mm howitzers were distributed to the 2e Régiment de Cuirassiers of the French 1st Armoured Division. There is evidence that at least two regiments of the French 5th Armoured Division obtained M4A1s (75) and M4A1s (76) to a limited extent before the conclusion of hostilities.

As we have seen, British armoured vehicle doctrine was quite different from American doctrine, being more oriented towards developing methods to counter enemy tank concentrations.

Each British armoured brigade consisted of three tank regiments, units that were actually the size of a battalion. The armoured regiment was in turn divided into three squadrons (A, B, C) and a headquarters. The regimental headquarters normally had four wagons (three of them were observation wagons for the benefit of the artillery, whose main armament was replaced by false wooden guns).

Each squadron was equipped with 15 medium tanks, divided into 5 troops (including the command troop, which was also equipped with observation tanks). Later, a structure centred on 4 troops of 4 tanks each was introduced. In addition to the specialised troops assigned to the 79th Armoured Division, the British deployed six armoured brigades equipped with Sherman tanks in the European theatre of war. Two of them were undivided: the 5th Guard Brigade was an important component of the Guard Armoured Division, the 29th was an integral part of the 11th Armoured Division. The regiments of the 7th Armoured Division (the famous Desert Rats), on the other hand, relied primarily on Cromwell tanks, although they had the usual Firefly equipment. The other four brigades (4th, 8th, 27th, 33rd) were independent units, assigned to corps and divisional commands according to contingent needs.

As of 1943, all British armoured divisions included in their staffs an armoured scout regiment, which at the time of the Normandy operations was equipped with Cromwell tanks. This was a new type of unit that was sometimes used as a fourth tank battalion. Although the British Army made use of several versions of the Sherman, it must be noted that they were often not all represented in the same formation at the same time.

In addition to the Firefly, the British employed models armed with the 75 mm piece such as the M4, M4A1, M4A2 and M4A4. At the beginning of 1945, the 11th British Armoured Division decommissioned its Shermans, replacing them with the new Comet tanks.

Canadian armoured units deployed on the European front, such as the 4th and 5th Divisions and the 1st and 2nd Brigades, were also fully equipped with Sherman, mostly M4A2, M4A4 and Firefly. Contrary to what might be expected, the Canadian armoured scout regiments did not have any Cromwells but were equipped exclusively with Shermans and Stuarts. The Czechoslovak and Polish armoured formations were organised, like the Canadian ones, according to British principles. The M4A4 and Firefly were the most popular Sherman variants in the Polish 1st Armoured Division.

When the front stabilised near the Meuse, the majority of these tanks were replaced by new M4A1s (76) w. Trained by the British and deployed in France in the last days of August 1944, the 1st Independent Czechoslovak Armoured Brigade was tasked with containing the sorties of the German garrison barricaded in Dunkirk. The two (later three) tank battalions of this unit came into line with the Cromwells, but it is known that the Czechoslovaks obtained at least 36 Sherman Firefly.

The Sherman's objective inferiority to the heavier German tanks of the latest generation did not have a significant impact on the course of the war. Other factors were more important than the technological gap. One of these was certainly the training of the tank crews: many inexperienced German crews were going to fill the frightening gaps in the ranks of the Panzerwaffe, caused by the long years of conflict Germany had endured.

The Sherman fully fulfilled its function due to the increasing quality of its crews and the development of new tactics. Thanks to its superior mobility, the American-made medium tank was able to outmanoeuvre the better-protected German panzers by striking them on their more vulnerable flanks. More mechanically reliable than its opponents and available in large numbers, the Sherman made an important contribution to Allied successes on the battlefields of north-west Europe.

TECHNICAL SPECIFICATIONS

Main armament:

- Cannon: 75 mm M3 (in early versions).
Ammunition: High explosive (HE) and armour-piercing (AP) projectiles, with a muzzle velocity of approximately 620 m/s. The gun was effective against light armoured vehicles and for infantry support, but proved ineffective against German heavy tanks such as the Tiger and Panther.
- 76 mm M1 cannon (later versions such as the M4A3E8), with a higher muzzle velocity (around 792 m/s) to cope with thicker armour.

Secondary armament:

-Co-axial machine gun: Browning M1919A4 7.62 mm (calibre .30).
-Hull gun: A second 7.62 mm Browning M1919A4 mounted in the front hull.
-Aircraft gun: Browning M2 12.7 mm (calibre .50) mounted on the turret for defence against enemy aircraft or infantry.

Armour:

-Thickness of the front armouring: Varies between 51 mm and 76 mm of cast or rolled steel.
-Lateral armouring: approx. 38 mm.
The armour was sloped to improve protection, but it was still vulnerable to powerful German guns, especially the 88mm cannon.

Propulsion and mobility:

Engine: Different engines were used depending on the variants. Initial versions were equipped with a Continental R975 C1 nine-cylinder, radial, air-cooled petrol engine with an output of around 400-450 hp. Later versions, such as the M4A3, were fitted with the more powerful 500 hp Ford GAA V8 petrol engine.

▲ Shermans with vertical spring suspensions (VVSS) suffered from inadequate mobility on soft ground due to the high ground pressure exerted by the tracks. To initially remedy the problem, the Americans devised so-called 'duck-bills', additional connectors for the track links, in order to widen their width. US NARA.

▲ Detail of the Sherman's track wheels.

▼ Sherman M4 Firefly on display at the George Patton Museum, Fort Knox, USA.

M4A1 medium tank named 'Berlin and back', of Co. B, 760th Tank Battalion, US Fifth Army, Italy, January 1944.

- Maximum speed: Approximately 38-48 km/h on the road, depending on the model and ground conditions.
- Autonomy: Approx. 160-240 km on the road with a full tank of fuel (approx. 660 litres of petrol).

Suspension:

- Vertical Volute Spring Suspension (VVSS): In early versions, they allowed decent mobility, but could be a little stiff on rough terrain.
- Horizontal Volute Spring Suspension (HVSS): In later versions (such as the M4A3E8 'Easy Eight'), the suspension was improved for better stability and ride comfort.

Dimensions and Weight:

- Length: approx. 5.84 m (with cannon included).
- Width: approx. 2.62 m.
- Height: approx. 2.74 m.
- Weight: Approx. 30-33 tonnes depending on model and modifications.

Crew:

Composed of five members:
- Commander
- Cannonier
- Servant
- Pilot
- Assistant pilot/radio operator.

Ammunition:

- Capacity of carrying 90-97 projectiles for the main gun (75 mm or 76 mm).
- About 4,750 rounds for the 7.62 mm machine guns.
- 300-500 rounds for the 12.7 mm anti-aircraft machine gun.

Communications:

- Equipped with an SCR 528 radio for internal and external communications on the battlefield.

Main variants:

- M4: The basic version, with 75 mm cannon and VVSS suspension.
- M4A1: Similar to the M4, but with a cast steel hull.
- M4A2: Version with General Motors 6046 diesel engine and used mainly by the Soviets.
- M4A3: Equipped with the Ford GAA V8 engine and preferred by American forces.
- M4A3E8 'Easy Eight': Version with HVSS suspension and 76 mm cannon.
- M4A4: Version with Chrysler Multibank engine.

Technical strengths:

- Ease of maintenance: the Sherman was designed to be easily repairable in the field.
- Adaptability: Rapid modifications made it possible to transform it into specialised vehicles (such as mine-clearing tanks, flamethrowers, self-propelled artillery, etc.).
- Reliability: The design was robust and generally well tested in different battle conditions and environments.

Technical weaknesses:

- Undersized armour and armament compared to the German heavy tanks: It was not able to take on Tiger or Panther tanks head-on without suffering significant losses.
- Vulnerability to fire: The use of petrol fuel, combined with a rather vulnerable internal architecture, made the Sherman prone to catch fire when hit.

M4A1 medium tank of the 756th Tank battalion, 5th army in Cassino, Italy, February 1944.

▲ Curious picture of the Sherman 'War Daddy II', an M4A1 tank captured by the Germans and tested here in the Kummersdorf test field. Behind it is an M3 tank. Courtesy Bundesarchiv-Wiki CC1.

▼ Landing at Anzio on 27 April 1944 by the 5th US Army: 1st Armored Division, 13th Armored Regiment, Sherman tanks disembark from an L.S.T. (Landing Ship Tank) Signal Photo. Anzio, 27 April 1944.

▲ An M4 from C Company, 68th Tank Battalion, 6th Armoured Division moving over muddy terrain. US NARA.

OPERATIONAL USE

As a result of the British armed forces' desperate need for armoured forces, in June 1942, while American troops were training with their first Sherman tanks in US camps, British forces suffered a heavy defeat at the hands of the Panzerarmee Afrika at Tobruk. On 20 June, President Franklin Roosevelt asked Winston Churchill if there was anything the US could do to help. Churchill did not hesitate and replied: 'Send us as many Sherman tanks as you can, and get them to the Middle East as soon as possible'. Roosesvelt thus decided to offer the Shermans their baptism of fire on African soil, supplying them to the British ally. It amounted to almost 300 vehicles; this number represented almost the entire Sherman production up to that time. The tanks were hastily collected, taken directly from factories and even from American units that were just beginning to use them for training. The timing was not the best, however, as the convoy with the tanks was partly sunk, along with almost a hundred tanks that ended up at the bottom of the sea...

NORTH AFRICAN FRONT

A second convoy was then sent to compensate for the lost tanks. The Shermans, once in Egypt, were quickly adapted for desert combat, with the addition of extra protection, such as sand skirts. The Sherman made its first battle debut in October 1942, during the famous Second Battle of El-Alamein, fought by the British Eighth Army against the Italo-Germans. Despite hasty preparation, with several crews receiving their tanks on the day of the battle, and a battle plan not without flaws, which sent them straight into the minefields, the M4's performance was mixed. It was only in December of the same year that

▲ The Sherman 'Eternity' was among the first to take land on the European continent. Pictured here with the 7th Army, just landed at Red Beach 2 on 10 July 1943, during the Allied invasion of Sicily.

C company M4A2 Sherman medium tank, 756th tank battalion 5th Army, Cassino, Italy, February 1944.

the vehicle was used by the Americans for the first time, during the Tunisian campaign near Tebourba. Here too, the inexperience of the crews and unfortunate tactical decisions caused heavy losses, without, however, calling into question the quality of the vehicle, which nevertheless still lagged behind the efficient German vehicles. In any case, they had proved superior to their parent, the M3 Grant. By the end of the African campaign, the M4 and M4A1 had become the standard tanks of the American armoured divisions, while the M3 Grant was transferred to the Allied forces of Free France. Over time, the M4 and M4A1 began to be gradually replaced by the more advanced M4A3, starting with the fall of Rome in the summer of 1944.

■ THE WAR IN EUROPE ITALY, FRANCE AND GERMANY

After the African campaign, the Sherman was the protagonist in almost every battle of World War II. Once the initial difficulties in its tactical employment were overcome, it proved to be a formidable vehicle. Among its strengths were its high mechanical reliability and ease of maintenance, which ensured high operational availability. In addition, its relatively small mass and size gave it agility and the ability to cross most bridges in Europe, unlike the heavier German tanks. Its armament was powerful enough to compete with the Panzer IV, often surpassing it, mainly due to the turret's rotational speed, which allowed it to fire first.

However, as the war progressed and German tanks evolved, so did the Sherman's shortcomings. The fearsome Tiger and Panther proved to be almost impenetrable opponents to its fire, while maintaining the ability to hit and destroy Shermans from long distances, exposing the limitations of the American tank against these deadly steel monsters. During the war, the US Army equipped as many as 16 armoured di-

▲ American forces in Italy with the now unfailing Sherman.

▲ A Sherman ended up in a creek and half tipped over, with the engineers engaged in its recovery.

▲ A Sherman reinforced with track plates on the front as additional protection. Model preserved at the Langenberg Liberation Memorial in Ede, Holland.

M4A1 medium tank, Co. F, 13th Armoured Regt., 1st Armored Division, named 'Frantic', Anzio, Italy, March 1944.

Medium tank M4A1 (75mm) Company F, 13th Armored Regiment, 1st Armored Division 'Old Ironsides' Rome area, Italy, June 1944.

visions and 65 independent tank battalions, making it the Sherman's main user. Initially, each armoured division had two regiments of three battalions each, with two M4 battalions and one mechanised infantry battalion. This organisation, however, was not welcomed by the generals, who complained of an excess of tanks and a shortage of infantry.

In 1943, the structure was revised: now each division had three tank battalions and three mechanised infantry battalions, with the exception of the 2nd and 3rd Armoured Divisions, which retained their original configuration throughout the war. In this new organisation, one tank battalion consisted of three companies of M4 Sherman and one of M3 Stuart. While the 1942 division had 232 Shermans, the 1943 division fielded only 186, reflecting the change in strategy.

After the North African campaign, the Sherman became the beating heart of the US armoured forces. Not only were they heavily employed by the US Army, but also by the British and the Allies, taking part in almost all the most decisive campaigns of the war. During the invasion of Sicily, the Sherman proved its worth. Alongside the American 2nd Armoured Division and the 753rd Tank Battalion, the Sherman was among the first to go into action at Gela, supporting the crucial battles that followed the landings. From there, the 2nd Armoured Division advanced rapidly towards Palermo, which it occupied on 17 July. The Sherman's Italian adventure did not end in Sicily. After the landing at Salerno, it was employed in some of the fiercest battles of the Italian campaign, beginning at Cassino, where German resistance turned the landscape into an inferno of ruins, and ending at Anzio, where the American 1st Armoured Division helped establish the valuable bridgehead. This division remained in Italy until the end of the conflict, accompanied by eight independent battalions equipped with Sherman. In Italy, the Sherman was not only a direct battle weapon, but also a versatile base for specialised vehicles. Amongst these, two adapted

▲ The tactical infantry-tank combination was a constant in the US Army, as this photo showing a platoon of infantrymen backed by heavy equipment in the newly liberated Normandy also demonstrates.

vehicles stood out: the Twaby Ark, a bridge-carrying vehicle, and the Sherman pocket-carrier. The Twaby Ark, which lacked a turret, lowered mobile ramps into trenches, allowing troops to pass over improvised bridges. The Twaby Ark, also deprived of the turret, carried huge bundles of wood on rails welded to its length. These bundles, once dropped into the ditches, filled them, creating safe passages for vehicles. Also at Montecassino, an iconic battle site of the Italian campaign, the Shermans fought alongside the Polish 2nd Armoured Brigade, once again demonstrating their versatility and endurance in one of the toughest and most costly campaigns of the Second World War.

■ THE NORMANDY LANDINGS AND THE CAMPAIGN IN FRANCE

The Shermans made their debut in France on 6 June 1944, landing with the first wave on D-Day. Several hundred Sherman DDs (duplex drives), already successfully tested during Operation Avalanche, were deployed in the historic invasion. These first tanks were joined in the following months by 15 armoured divisions and 39 independent battalions, with the M4 in its many variants forming the backbone of these formations. However, on the European battlefield, the Sherman was entirely confronted with its limitations. In particular, the confrontation with the more advanced Panzer V revealed the weaknesses of the American tank, which could not compete in terms of firepower and armour. Nevertheless, the Shermans operated alongside other Allied forces, especially on the Western Front, alongside British, French and Polish troops. In the French forces, the Shermans served with distinction in the 2nd Armoured Division, led by General Leclerc, which was the first unit to return triumphantly to Paris in 1944. The French 1st and 5th Armoured Divisions were also equipped with these tanks. On the Polish front, however, the 1st Armoured Division, part of the Allied forces, managed to distinguish itself as the first to enter Wilhelmshaven.

▲ M4A2 Sherman of the American armoured divisions land in Normandy in August 1944.

M4 medium tank (75mm) of the 5th Armored Division. This unit played a primary role in the sacking of the Crag and the subsequent advance towards Paris in the summer of 1944.

In addition to the West, the Shermans also operated on the Eastern Front. The Red Army received as many as 4,102 of them (2007 M4A2s and 2095 M4A2s with 76 mm cannon), and these tanks helped break through the German lines, pushing as far as Berlin and Budapest. Among the most prestigious Soviet units equipped with the Sherman was the 3rd Guards Mechanised Corps. M4A2 commander V.A. Galkin, a member of the 31st Tank Regiment, was awarded the honour of 'Hero of the Soviet Union' for his valour in battle.

▪ WAR IN THE PACIFIC

In the early stages of the war in the Pacific, as in the Guadalcanal campaign, the US Marine Corps deployed M2A4 light tanks against the Japanese, who were using their Type 95 Ha-Go. Both vehicles were equipped with 37 mm cannons, but even the M2A4 alone, produced in 1940, was about five years more technologically advanced than its Japanese opponent.

In 1943, the Imperial Japanese Army, however, continued to employ Type 95 and Type 97 Chi-Has, while the Allied forces began to replace their light tanks with the more powerful M4 Sherman, armed with 75 mm cannons. Chinese forces, equipped with 100 Shermans in the China-Burma-India theatre, also used them with remarkable effectiveness in the offensives of 1944 and 1945. This offered a devastating advantage to American forces and their allies in the Pacific.

In an attempt to counter the Sherman, the Japanese developed two new tanks: the Type 3 Chi-Nu and the heavier Type 4 Chi-To, both equipped with 75 mm cannons, but of different designs. However, production was limited to only 166 Type 3s and two Type 4s, and none of these vehicles ever saw combat, having been retained for the defence of the Japanese islands. Thus, the Japanese had to rely once again on 1930s tanks to face the increasingly modern Allied armoured vehicles produced in the 1940s.

▲ The famous Sherman symbol of resistance in the Battle of the Ardennes: 'First in Bastogne'.

In the final years of the war, the Allies discovered that high-explosive munitions were more effective against Japanese tanks, as armour-piercing projectiles, designed to penetrate thicker armour, easily passed through the Type 95 Ha-Go's thin armour without causing significant damage.

While the high-velocity guns of the tank destroyers were useful against well-constructed fortifications, M4 Shermans armed with flamethrowers often proved more suitable, as conventional fire was rarely sufficient to eliminate Japanese trenches and bunkers.

▲ Kwajalein Atoll. A soldier posing in front of the Sherman 'Killer' on which a captured Japanese Type 94 light tank was placed. Right: an M4A3 flamethrower version during the Battle of Iwo Jima.

▲ A platoon of Sherman tanks of the 713th Armoured Battalion assembled on a ridge in Okinawa.

▲ View of the M4 Sherman tank from above.

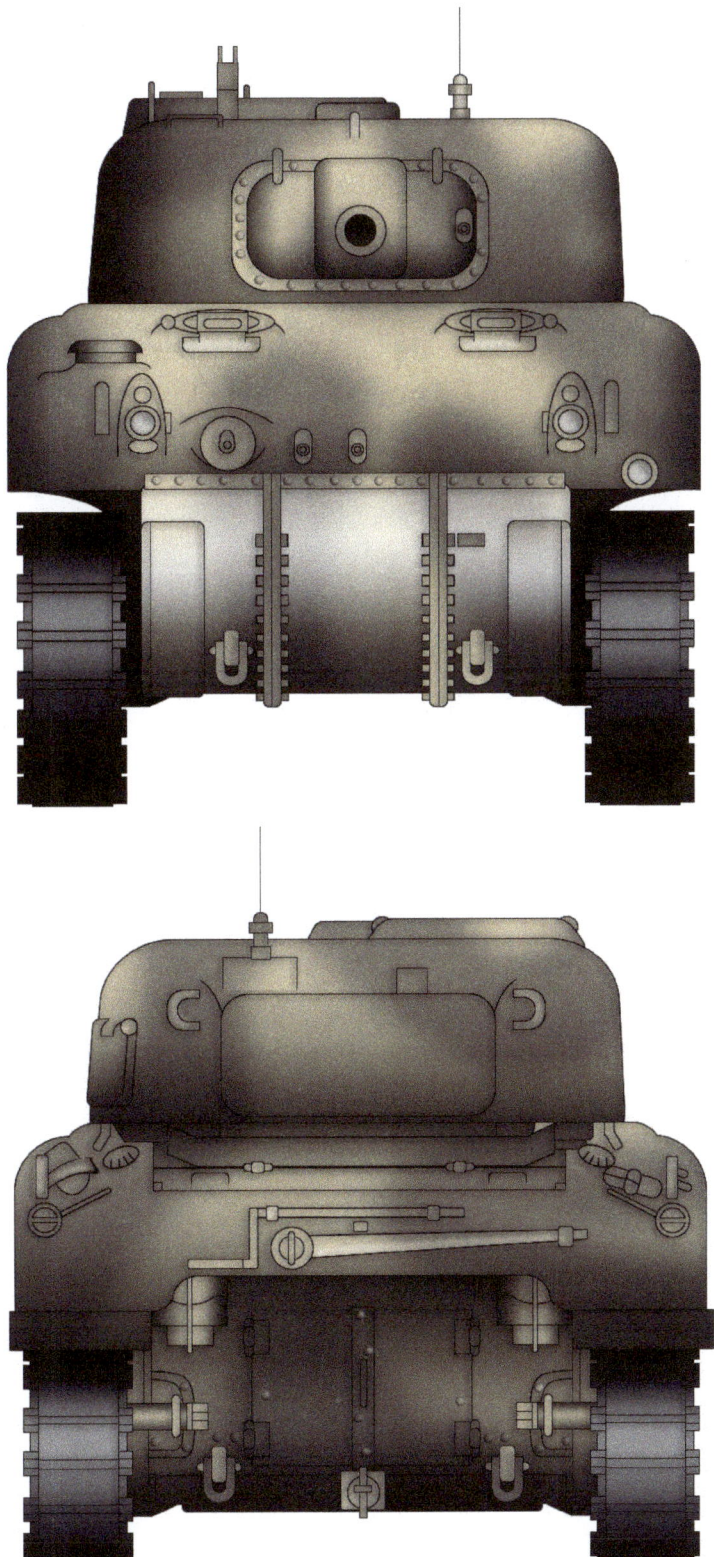

▲ Front and rear view of the M4 Sherman tank.

M4 medium tank (75mm) 32nd Armored Regiment - Normandy, France, July 1944. M4 equippagged with Culin device for combat in the French bocage.

KOREAN WAR

During the Korean War, the Sherman M4A3E8, also known as the 'Easy Eight', was the US Army's main battle tank until the Armistice Agreement was signed. At the beginning of the conflict, the US Army aimed to deploy the M4A3E8 to counter the powerful Russian-supplied North Korean T-34-85. However, due to the post-World War II disarmament, there was limited availability of tanks ready for rapid deployment from the Far East.

The US Far Eastern Command recovered 58 M4A3E8s that were in Japan, creating the 8072nd Temporary Tank Battalion (later renamed the 89th Tank Battalion) on 17 July. These tanks were landed at Busan on 1 August and immediately deployed in the Battle of Masan, supporting the 25th US Infantry Division.

In 1950, a total of 679 M4A3E8s were deployed on the Korean Peninsula. Although the M4A3E8 and the T-34-85 were comparable and capable of annihilation at normal combat ranges, the use of high velocity armour piercing (HVAP) ammunition, advanced optics and superior crew training gave the Sherman a strategic advantage. Between July and November 1950, the M4A3E8, armed with 76mm HVAP ammunition, destroyed 41 enemy tanks.

However, the M4A3E8 had a lower anti-tank combat capability than larger calibre tanks such as the M26 Pershing and M46 Patton, which were operational at the same time. Despite this, the lighter M4A3E8 became the tank of choice for the United States in the later stages of the conflict due to its superior manoeuvrability over rough terrain and ease of maintenance, supported by good mechanical reliability. These characteristics made it particularly effective in providing close support to infantry units, especially

▲ American Sherman tanks in a lull during the Korean conflict.

during operations in high and mountainous terrain. Starting in December 1951, around 20 M4A3E8s were assigned to the Marine Corps of the Republic of Korea, while the US Army employed M36 GMCs as its main armoured vehicle during the conflict.

Towards the middle of the war, the Australian Army judged the Grant to be unsuitable for overseas war tasks and the units that had used the M3 tank were re-equipped with the Matilda II before being deployed in the New Guinea and Borneo Campaigns. Due to personnel shortages, all three divisions were officially disbanded in 1943 and downsized to brigade and battalion level units.

▲ A flame-throwing Sherman tank fires a volley of napalm during training manoeuvres during the September 1953 peace talks in Korea.

▲ Sherman M-4 Tiger Tank, during the offensive launched by the 5th Rct against North Korean forces. Korea 1951. Right: Loading a Sherman onto a USMC at the Naval Suppy Center Oakland in 1950.

M4 medium tank (75 mm) 37th Tank Battalion, Command Company, 4th Armoured Division Normandy, France, August 1944.

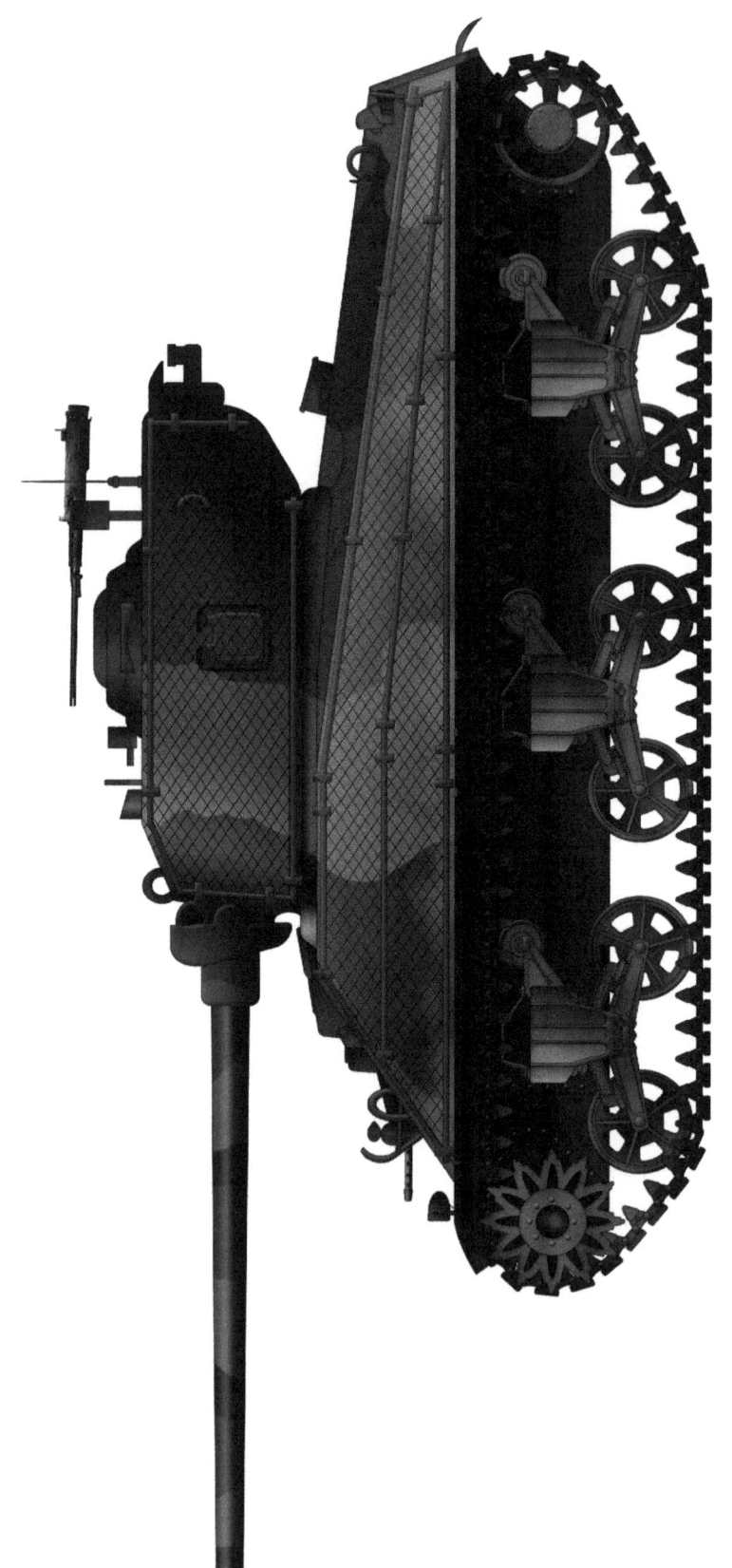

M4A3 Medium Tank (76mm), of the 19th Tank Battalion, 9th Armored Division, Belgium, November 1944.

CAMOUFLAGE AND DISTINCTIVE MARKS

During World War II, the US Army Corps of Engineers was responsible for the camouflage of military vehicles and developed a whole series of manuals (FM) and other instructions for this purpose. The purpose of these manuals was to instruct the leaders of the Engineer Battalions to use these colours appropriately and to adopt the camouflage patterns indicated.

The two most significant manuals were FM 5-20 and FM 5-21, published in October 1942. During the war, the US Army Engineer Corps specified several colours, which we quote here along with their Federal Standard Equivalent:

- No. 9 Olive Drab
- No. 22 Olive Drab
- No. 8 Earth Red
- No. 6 Earth Yellow
- No. 5 Earth Brown
- No. 1 Light Green
- No. 31 Olive Drab (olive green)
- No. 11 Forest Green
- No. 10 Black
- No. 12 Desert Sand,
- Ocean Gray
- Olive Drab 50 (dark olive green).

The background colour par excellence, which came into being in the 1930s, was Olive Drab (OD) No. 22. The same one that later became No. 9 from 1942. Olive Drab in the broadest sense had been the basic colour in the USA since 1917.

The shade of Olive Drab used by the USAAF was darker than that of the Army and was designated as Olive Drab No. 31. This shade was not unified with the Army's because it had a specific anti-infrared characteristic.

The Olive Drab colour shades underwent several changes during the course of the war, but not the colour specifications, which remained unchanged since the 1920s. In the years leading up to the Second World War, the colours appeared in an opaque tone, while by the end of the war it had evolved into a more satin-like tone, almost glossy in some cases.

The colour also changed in brightness; at the beginning of the war the shade was lighter than at the end of the war. Variations were also due to the different paint manufacturers, who had different shades of Olive Drab, ranging from yellow to brown. As already mentioned, the Olive Drab used towards the end of the war had a sheen characteristic and the shade was more brown, making for a very different hue from that seen at the outbreak of the Second World War.

The Marine Corps used colours more complementary to those used by the Army, such as colour No. 12 Desert Sand to camouflage their vehicles, as well as all the OD, Earth Yellow and Earth Red colour variants.

The Marine Corps, like the army, used Forest Green as the base colour for its M3 and M2A2 tanks, but never used the OD colour for the same vehicles. Also among the marines, some LVTPs and landing craft were painted in a grey colour called Ocean Grey.

The Army had a battalion that specialised in painting vehicles, while the Marine Corps relied on the vehicle crews to apply the paint and any camouflage. This practice soon spread throughout the Corps,

COLORI E MIMETICHE ESERCITO AMERICANO (USA) WW2

Insignia White	Ocean Grey	White	Aged White	Ivory	US Sand	US Light Green
US Field Drab	US Olive Drab	US Forrest Green	US Earth Red	US Earth Brown	Black	UK Tommy Green

and the Marines took pride in it, as it allowed them some 'artistic' freedom in creating their camouflage. During the Solomon Islands invasion, some very colourful camouflage models appeared.

In the army, the 1st Armoured Division was the first armoured unit deployed in Africa. Its vehicles were painted in Olive Drab, with large yellow stripes and stars. So flashy that the Germans called these tanks 'ideal targets'. In fact, during the first battles against the German forces it was soon realised that these colours were not a good choice in the desert environment. Consequently, American troops began using local sand and paint to camouflage their vehicles in the North African environment.

■ LAST PERIOD

It was only after the invasion of Sicily, otherwise known as Operation Husky, that the formal colours established by the Corps of Engineers were also used to camouflage vehicles in Africa. It was then that the complementary colours Earth Yellow No. 6 and Earth Red No. 8 began to be used.

Vehicles and armoured vehicles that operated in forests and hot climates had to be painted in Olive drab 50 and Black; both dark colours applied in a large stripe pattern. Later, light green No. 1 was also added as a complementary colour. White was obviously used for camouflage in cold and arctic climates.

COLORI E MIMETICHE ESERCITO INGLESE WW2

Silver Grey Afrika-Balkan	Slate Afrika-Balkan	Light Stone Afrika-Balkan	Portland Stone Afrika-Balkan	Desert Pink Afrika-Balkan	Dark Olive Afrika-Balkan	Dark Gun Metal
Olive Drab Disruptive Europe	Blue Black Disruptive Europe	Light Mud Disruptive Europe	Brown Disruptive Europe	Dark Brown Disruptive Europe	Deep Bronze Green Disruptive Europe	Tommy Green

M4A1 (75) Sherman medium tank (late model) 31st Tank Battalion (C Company), 7th Armoured Division 'Lucky Seventh' Saint-Vith, Belgium, December 1944.

▲▼ American troops, together with their Shermans, proceed to conquer German towns in 1945.

M4A3 medium tank (75 mm Jumbo assault gun) C Company, 37th Tank Btg, 4th Armoured Division Bastogne, Belgium, December 1944

Medium tank M4A3 (76), named 'Kokomo', of the commander of the 760th Tank Battalion, US Fifth Army, Northern Italy, January 1945.

VERSIONS OF THE VEHICLE

The M4 Sherman, the US Army's iconic World War II tank, experienced a numerous series of variants developed in response to wartime requirements and engine production limitations. The Whirlwind, an aircraft engine used in the early models, was also requested by the USAAF (United States Army Air Force), which prompted the exploration of engine alternatives to ensure continued production of the tank.

These are the main variants of the Sherman and their characteristics:

-**M4 (Sherman I):** The basic model, the M4, was equipped with a 9-cylinder Continental R975 radial engine, capable of developing 380 HP. Its welded hull and external features, such as air filter housings and rear armour, made it instantly recognisable. Production of this model began in July 1942 and involved numerous companies to meet the high demand. A total of 6,748 units with a 75-mm cannon were produced.

-**M4A1 (Sherman II):** To overcome the complexity of welding hulls, the M4A1 was the first Sherman to feature a cast hull with rounded corners. It shared the engine with the M4 and was produced in about 6,281 examples with 75 mm cannon and 3,426 with 76 mm cannon.

▲ Famous picture showing the first Sherman landing on the beach at Anzio, Italy 1944.

-M4A2 (Sherman III): Due to the shortage of Whirlwind engines, the GM Twin 6-71 diesel engine was introduced. This model was mainly used by the Allied nations as part of the Lend-Lease programme, as the US Army preferred petrol-powered tanks to avoid logistical problems. Over 8,000 were built with a hull similar to the M4.

-M4A3 e M4A3W (Sherman IV): The powerful and reliable Ford GAA engine made this variant a favourite. Equipped with 500 HP, it was recognisable by cooling grilles on the bonnet and an elongated rear plate. The M4A3W version, with water-protected ammunition to reduce the risk of fire, became the US Army standard, remaining in service after the war.

-M4(105) e M4A3(105): These models, armed with a 105 mm howitzer, were intended for close infantry support. Some 4,680 examples were built between 1944 and 1945.

-M4A1(76) W e M4A3(76) W: Both variants adopted a new T23 turret, which housed a 76 mm long gun, offering superior firepower.

-M4A3E2 Jumbo: A variant with reinforced armour, designed to open the way for columns during ambush missions. 254 examples were built, some of which were later rearmed with 76 mm cannons.

-M4A3E8 (Easy Eighth): Known for its HVSS suspension system, which improved mobility and comfort over rough terrain, the 'Easy Eight' model was one of the stars of the Korean War. It was equipped with a 76mm cannon.

-M4A4 (Sherman V): This variant mounted the Chrysler A-57 engine, a 30-cylinder engine that required the hull to be lengthened. This model was mainly built for the British Army.

-M4 Calliope: Finally, the Sherman Calliope incorporated a rocket launcher device, turning it into a mobile artillery vehicle, capable of hitting armoured and infantry targets. It existed in two variants: the short-range T40 Whizbang and the long-range T34 Calliope.

In conclusion, the variety of versions of the Sherman reflects the adaptability of this tank to the battlefield requirements and production challenges of the time. Thanks to this flexibility, the Sherman remained a major player in 20th century armoured warfare.

▲ An M4A3 tank with side plates for ammunition protection. Wiki CC1.

▲ Evolution of the Sherman M4 tank up to the Korean War. Courtesy by NotLessOrEqual CC1.

▲ Various pictures of the Sherman M4 tank on display at the Novegro exhibition park (Italy). Photo author.

Recovery tank M4 (75 mm) 175th Tank Bttn, 123rd Rgt, 33rd Infantry Division - Philippines, March 1945.

CONCLUSIONS

Summing up, the M Sherman was a perfect example of how mass production and reliability can often overcome sheer technical superiority. While German tanks like the Tiger and Panther were more powerful in terms of armament and armour, they were also expensive, complex to produce and difficult to maintain.

The Sherman, on the other hand, was lighter, easier to produce and maintain and, above all, available in huge numbers. This was achieved mainly due to its relatively simple design, which ultimately required far fewer resources than the German tanks. The Allies were able to exploit this numerical and logistical advantage to overcome the German forces, despite the tank's limitations. It was also a vehicle with high mechanical reliability, being able to cover large stretches and distances without suffering significant breakdowns. Another major advantage was easy maintenance: the Sherman was designed to be easy to repair and maintain in the field. Spare parts were plentiful and crews could often carry out repairs quickly, a crucial aspect in keeping the vehicles operational.

Not to forget mobility: Although it was not the fastest wagon, the Sherman had a good overall range thanks to a powerful engine and a good power-to-weight ratio. It was suitable for a variety of terrains, which allowed it to operate profitably in Europe, North Africa and the Pacific.

The vehicle also proved to be very flexible: the Sherman was used in numerous variants, adapted as a tank destroyer, mobile artillery, flamethrower and other specialised roles, demonstrating its versatility. Ultimately, the Sherman was not the best tank in terms of power or protection, but it was perhaps the most effective and decisive in the Allied victory due to its reliability, adaptability and the fact that it could be produced in large quantities.

DATA SHEET	
	Sherman M4
Length	5840 mm
Width	2620 mm
Height	2740 mm
Date of entry into service/exit	1942/1955
Weight in combat order	30,3 t
Crew	5 (commander, pilot, servants and gunner)
Engine	Continental R-975-EC1 petrol, Ford GAA V8 and others
Maximum speed	48 km/h on road 22 km/h off road
Autonomy	193 km on road, 160 off road
Maximum slope	34,5%
Unit cost	From $44,000 to $65,000 equal to 600-800,000 euro today
Armament	1 M3 L/40 75 mm gun 1 Browning M2HB cal. 50 machine gun 2 Browning M1919A4 cal .30 (7.62 mm) machine guns
Production	49.300

M4A3 medium tank Flame Marines corps 4th tank battalion at Jwo Jma, Japan, March 1945. Note the rear vents to provide air to the cockpit even while ditching for landing.

MAIN USERS

Nation	Quantity	Notes
Argentina		
Australia		Test proposals only
Brasil	80 M4	
Canada		The last were withdrawn in 1970
Chile		
Cuba		
China		
South Korea	12	In service since 1950
Denmark		M4E4 (76mm)
Egypt		Used between 1947 and 1956
France	1.254 M4A1 (76mm)	In service from 1943 to 1967
Filippines		
Japan	264 M4A3E8	Retired in the late 1970s
Israel		In service from 1947 to 1970
India		
Italy	M4, M4A1, M4A2 ed M4A4	From 1947 to 1952
Lebanon		Supplied by Israel
New Zealand		
Holland	44	Since 1952
Poland		
Portugal	M4E4 (76mm)	
Uganda		Supplied by Israele
Pakistan	547 (year 1950) nad 40 (1971)	M4E4 (76mm)
Paraguay		Withdrawn in 2018
UK	17.184	Including the vehicles provided to the Commonwealth
URSS	2.007 M4A2 75 et 2.095 M4A2(76)	In service between 1944 and 1945
USA	More than 20.000	In service until 1954
Jugoslavia	599	M4E4 (76mm) supplied between 1951 and 1957

After the end of the Second World War, Sherman tanks were distributed to various NATO armies, continuing to serve for both US forces and their allies during the Korean War. Years later, they were handed over to the Israeli army, which, seeking a technological upgrade, decided to modify them by installing the CN-75-50 L/61.5 75 mm gun from the French AMX-13/75 light tank and the powerful 105 mm Modèle F1 from the AMX-30, a French battle tank. These modified versions, known as the M-50 and M-51, were dubbed the 'Super Sherman' and demonstrated how a vehicle now considered obsolete could be renewed for frontline use. Super Shermans played an important role during the Six-Day War in 1967, and in the Yom Kippur War in 1973. However, with the advent of the more modern Merkava tank, the M-50 and M-51 were eventually withdrawn from active Israeli service in 1980.

Colonel Creighton Abrhams' M4 "Thunderbolts VII" medium tank and his famous personal insignia, Horazdovice, Czechoslovakia, May 1945.

M4 A2 Medium Tank (75mm) of the 6th Tank Battalion, US Marine Corps - Naha Sector, Okinawa, June 1945.

▲ Propaganda posters of the American tank workshops.

BIBLIOGRAPHY

- Bishop, Chris *The Encyclopedia of Weapons of World War II* (2002) Metro Books.
- Calderon e Fernandez, *Sherman the American miracle,* spain 2017
- Chamberlain, Peter; Ellis, Chris. *British and American Tanks of World War II.* New York: Arco.
- Culver B. "Sherman in Action", Squadron/Signal Publications, 1977.
- Doyle David, *Sherman Tank: America's M4 and M4, 105, Medium Tanks in World War II*
- Esteve Michel, Sherman: *The M4 Tank in World War II* Casematte pubblisher
- Fletcher D., "Sherman Firefly", Osprey Publishing Ltd., 2008.
- Ford Roger, *The Sherman Tank: Weapons of War* , History press UK
- Forty G. "United States Tanks of World War II", Blandford Press, 1989.
- Gawrych Wojcisch, *M4A2 Sherman Part 1.* Armor photogallery
- Gawrych Wojcisch, *M4 Sherman WC Firefly.* Armor photogallery
- Askew Michael, *M4 Sherman Tanks: The Illustrated History of America's Most Iconic Fighting Vehicles*
- Hunnicutt, R. P. Sherman, *A History of the American Medium Tank.* 1978; Taurus Enterprises.
- Mesko J., "Walk Around M4 Sherman", Squadron/Signal Publications, 2000.
- Mokva Stanislaw, *M4 Sherman: M4, M4A1, M4A4 Firefly,* Kagero
- Oliver Dennis, *Sherman tanks US army in Europe 1944-1945*
- Porter, David *Allied Tanks of World War II (World's Great Weapons)* (2014) Amber Books
- Sandars J. "The Sherman Tank in British Service 1942-45", Osprey Publishing, 1982.
- Stansell P., Laughlin K., "Son of Sherman Vol. 1: The Sherman Design and Development", The Ampersand Group, 2013.
- USMC D-F Series Tables of Equipment (TOEs), 1942-1944.
- White B. T., "British Tanks and Fighting Vehicles 1914-1945" Ian Allan Ltd., 1970.
- War departement, *M4 Sherman Medium Tank Crew Manual*
- Ware Pat, *M4 Sherman: Entwicklung, Technik, Einsatz*
- Ware Pat, *Char Sherman: Toutes les variantes du M4 depuis 1941*
- Zaloga, Steven (2008). *Armored Thunderbolt: The US Army Sherman in World War II.* Stackpole Books. ISBN 978-0-8117-0424-3.
- Zaloga S. J., "Armored Thunderbolt: The U.S. Army Sherman in World War II", Stackpole Books, 2008.
- Zaloga S. J., "M4 (76mm) Sherman Medium Tank 1943-65", Osprey Publishing, 2003.
- Zaloga S. J., "Patton's Tanks", Arms and Armour Press, 1984
- Zaloga S. J., "Sherman Medium Tank 1942-1945", Osprey Publishing, 1993.
- Zaloga S. J., *The Sherman at war, US army in Europe* Concord Publishing.

ALREADY PUBLISHED

ALL BOOKS IN THE SERIES ARE PRINTED IN ITALIAN AND ENGLISH

VISIT OUR WEBSITE FOR MORE INFORMATION ON
THE WEAPONS ENCYCLOPAEDIA:
https://soldiershop.com/collane/libri/the-weapons-encyclopaedia/

TWE-030 EN

www.ingramcontent.com/pod-product-compliance
Lightning Source LLC
LaVergne TN
LVHW072122060526
838201LV00068B/4949